BRITAIN IN COLOUR

Introduction and Commentaries by R. M. Lockley

BRITAIN

in colour

B. T. BATSFORD LTD London

First published, 1964

Reprinted, 1967, 1969

7134 0016 1

PRINTED IN THE NETHERLANDS BY DE LANGE/VAN LEER N.V., DEVENTER
FOR THE PUBLISHERS
B. T. BATSFORD LTD
4 FITZHARDINGE STREET, PORTMAN SQUARE, LONDON, W.1.

Contents

Introduction

Although of no great area the British Isles are so full of contrasting scenes, and variations of land-use, so packed with evidence of centuries of the history of man, that there is never monotony in any day's journey through the landscape. The discovered story of the peoples in these islands is satisfyingly ancient in origin, excitingly diverse in telling. In the records of the Saxons and the writings of the Romans, the land was inhabited by Britons or Brythons. That description has persisted to the present day. The majority of us think of the archipelago as the British Isles.

Even the Southern Irish, who prefer to call themselves Irish of the Republic of Eire, cannot escape the fact that they are British. We shall presently explain why. The island of Ireland was once united under one parliament, held in the halls of Tara, fourteen hundred years ago, but since then that political wholeness has been shattered. The six counties of Northern Ireland adhere to, and are racially and economically part of, Great Britain, with representatives in the British parliament in London. This book covers these six counties of Ulster, as well as all England, Wales and Scotland, all those parts of these islands which in fact come under the crown of Elizabeth II. To the world this union between the four regions inhabited by the four races of English, Welsh, Scotch and Northern Irish peoples is known as the United Kingdom.

What a lesson for us in international goodwill and humility an examination of three thousand years of history ought to be! For it ought to show the British that their origins, of which they are sometimes too consciously proud, are no better than those of many a newer nation; that they are composite of vanquished races and tribes, century by century accepting the will of their conquerors, who in turn have become absorbed or conquered or both. Each new invader from the lean eastern lands brought his fierce will to dominate for a while, to add new blood to the sluggish circulation of the cross-breed settler whose life of peace had turned the sharp sword of adventure into the dull ploughshare of security.

The British people are an amalgam of the blood of Silurian, Iberian, Celt, Roman, Saxon, Viking, Norman—to name the succession of invaders since the islands emerged as such from the continent of Europe after the last glaciation, which left the plain of England open to settlement, where "the untamed forest was king". It cannot be denied that the modern Englishman is a mongrel, albeit a proud one; but the Welshman is still half a Celt, and the Scotsman a mixture of Gaelic Celt and Viking. In this book we shall see the signs of the comings and goings of these races in a landscape rich with the evidence, with earthworks, cromlechs, dolmens, stone circles, stone fortress and wall, castle, defended house, ancient religious buildings, the houses of these peoples. To those whose sense of history is strong this visible heritage is deeply satisfying; they will hear the faint echoes of warriors at battle, of kings crowned, of chieftains deposed, priests at prayer, the singing of waves mingled with the cry of alien voices of invaders beaching their plundering ships of war.

It is well known that climate makes character. The Roman historian remarked on the mild winters of Britain, the sky overcast with cloud and rain. The equable climate produced the equable British character, softer and most English in the warmer south, tougher in the cooler north, more tempestuous in the wild windswept mountains of Wales. For history is the handmaiden of geography. Nations are moulded into mood and shape by the physical limits of seas and mountains.

The mountainous west and north of Britain became the refuge of those early settlers who were driven from the rich earth and mature forests of the southern and eastern plains by the sea-faring nomads from eastern Europe. Momentarily safe in their fastness the dispossessed tribes, grouped in families related by blood and with their captured slaves, instead of combining against the invader, often fought to the death, clan against clan, in a desperate territorial struggle to carve a living from the infertile mountains and glens.

Now it is a strange fact that the original Celt, like the Saxon and Viking who followed his migration west, was tall and fair-haired. Yet most of the Welsh and Irish whom you meet today are like their pre-Celtic dark-haired ancestors, which for want of a better title we call Iberians—those Mediterranean colonists who brought the art of the stone tomb and circle to the British Isles. The dark-haired Iberian type survives at its purest in England only in the Lake District and Cornwall; and in Wales and western Ireland. The infusion of the restless fair-haired peoples was insufficient to change much the dark Mediterranean blood which, by long centuries of acclimatisation, had become adapted to survive in the remote west. It is also said that the dark-haired people were more prolific breeders than the fair-heads, although on what statistical evidence we do not know. But here and there a fair-head or a red-head reappears today in the darkest Welsh or Irish family to remind us of that Celtic infusion.

This pattern of invasion of the low fertile plain of England by succeeding tribes of plundering fair-heads—Celt, Anglo-Saxons, Viking and Norman—and their failure to extirpate the aboriginal people of the misty mountains and islands of the west, is the key to understanding the character of the people of Britain. While the universal language of commerce between Britons is English, that most ancient of European languages—Brythonic or Welsh—is still freely spoken in the country homes of Wales; and it lives vigorously in the Welsh programmes of the B.B.C. You may also hear a form of Welsh spoken in the north-west of France by the Bretons of Brittany—the numerals for example are identical. It has died out in Cornwall—except that a written version lives in the literature there. Shepherds of the Lake District used to, and may still, count in Welsh; it was from the Lake District that the Welsh chieftain Cunedda about the year 500 descended upon North Wales and became head of the kingly house of that name which is so much revered in Welsh history.

The official language of Eire is Erse, itself a close relation of Gaelic, the "national" language of Scotland; both derived from the Celtic Goidels who preceded the Celtic Brythons. Only in the far west of Scotland and Ireland are Gaelic and Erse respectively in common use; although Erse is being revived vigorously in schools in Eire. English likewise is derived from a mixture of related languages from the fair-headed invaders of the east: the Angles, Saxons, Norse and Normans.

Yet if English is the common language of Britain today the dominating influence in commerce and even world affairs is far from being exclusively English. Scotch, Irish and Welsh surnames figure as leaders in these spheres equally with names of Saxon and Norman derivation, as they do in U.S.A., Canada, Australia and New Zealand, the principal overseas English-speaking nations. Again the Celtic dark-haired people, with their noted ability to breed and their quick impulsive natures, are swift to seize opportunity and go forth into the world to earn a competence; economic circumstance is the driving force, as it is with the more cautious level-headed Scot. It is a one-way traffic or migration, a movement of surplus population into England and abroad, infusing the English-speaking world with dynamic Celtic and Gaelic blood. There is no compensatory movement of English people into the Celtic lands, although these have become very much the holiday playground of English people, and for the good reason that these are so grand and beautiful scenically.

There still remain old frontiers to the speech of Angle, Saxon, Norman and other English root languages, in the various and diverse dialects which you will meet up and down the length and breadth of Britain. This is especially noticeable in contact with the land, where the names of animals and farm objects differ, as foreign languages, from one county to another. The Cockney with harsh and lively London accent, can hardly understand the soft zizzing English of the Devon and Somerset countryman. The "Oxford accent" is noted for its epiglottal haughtiness, considered by strangers as an affectation. Lancashire and Yorkshire express their dialect with a witty sharp resonance or twang. Cornwall has elements of her many settlers—metallic, Mediterranean.

In Scotland too there are strange ways of speaking English: the Lowland way of pursed lips immortalised by Burns; and the broad Highland brogue; both have spread across the world with colonising Scots, and I have met them just as powerful and hard to understand in the south of New Zealand. In the age of rationalisation one prays that the smooth "correct" voice of trained B.B.C. commentators will not have too depressing an effect on these pleasant diversities of the English language.

And what of a roof to live under? This book will not illustrate much that is new in architecture. It is not the purpose of this preface to groan over the rebuilding of English cities on the lines of New York. Until man settles the problem of overpopulation by adequate birth-control our economy must continue to expand (in the catchphrase of the politician) in order to provide work and housing for increasing millions of citizens. We can only hope that modern planning will not obliterate so much that is beautiful and irreplaceable in Britain. Our purpose rather is to show that much remains to make this country worth living in, and worth special effort to preserve. And we can all strive towards that preservation. Britain will become a dull ant-heap if we continue to smother the country with concrete. Then truly we shall live by bread alone, and our souls miserably perish for lack of vision to protect the unique heritage of a landscape glorious with its variety of mellowed villages and farms, historic buildings, and mountain, lake, river and island scenery.

LONDON

London is already large enough. Here and there another giant modern skyscraper soars upwards, and in its lofty isolation is not unbeautiful at moments when its windows flash in the sun of a soft English day. More, however, we do not wish to see. Londoners love their ancient city; and we hope will not easily allow its treasures to be buried in the shadows of the concrete canyons of commerce without strong resistance.

London's history is a stirring one. The town began, it is said, with the Roman settlement; but as a village it may date earlier. Its name is Celtic; in modern Welsh perhaps *Llyn-dain*, "Pool-fortress". Its name may have been given by Shakespeare's Cymbeline, a British chieftain of the Catuvellauni tribe living at peace with the Romans. This was the century of Christ's birth, of Julius Caesar's murder. At the time of Queen Boudicca (Boadicea) of the Iceni, Tacitus described London as "packed with traders and a celebrated centre of commerce". Ill-treated by the Romans who exploited, plundered and confiscated freely, Boudicca razed London by fire in A.D. 60, and slaughtered and gibbetted its inhabitants. The Roman reprisal took the form of a massacre which removed the Iceni from history altogether. Boudicca took

poison; her East Anglian lands were derelict for several generations.

The Romans protected London with a stone fortress, and the Wall of London was begun about this period. It was built so strongly that parts of it survive today. It enclosed over 300 acres of ground, and *Londinium* was thus the largest town in Britain, containing probably around 30,000 souls. Portions of the Wall listed as visible today include bastions of the wall at the Tower of London, and other sections at the General Post Office, St Giles Cripplegate (site of the Roman fortress) and seven other places. Roman finds have been unearthed frequently during building operations. The discovery in 1954 of the famous Temple of Mithras, with its broken statuary, provided the archaeological sensation of the year.

The Romans departed in the year 410. Their temples, desecrated and deserted, were torn down for building materials. St Paul's Cathedral (17) was founded in 604 with ample use of Roman stone, and rebuilt again after 1080. But the Anglo-Saxon influence on London is hardly visible today. The wooden town was sacked and burnt in the ninth and tenth centuries, and until well after the Norman occupation there was no firm peace. The population seems to have declined—in 1380 a poll tax suggests about 20,000 souls. Fire and plague continued to visit London, up to the Great Fire of 1666. But after each visitation Londoners rebuilt; as they did after the 1940-5 devastation of the second Great War. London proved itself indestructible.

It is this sense of history and phoenix-like resilience that gives one a warm feeling of fondness and faith in the old city, which is the very heart of British civilisation. And on a fine day in spring there is nothing to equal the soft English light bathing the venerable buildings, the busy river of little ships (23), and the new-leafed plane trees of the parks and squares (25).

London parks are the tidy remnant of the forested spaces of the pre-Roman occupation, outside the walls of the early fortress and of the present city. Westminster Abbey is the church of this outer western part of London, on the site of an earlier church (21). It was rebuilt by Edward the Confessor. Norman London had already overflowed the Wall, and even the Norman fortress of the Tower of London lies outside the old City. So does Westminster

Palace, the seat of government since Norman times, and now accommodating both Houses of Parliament (23). And it is in this other city, Westminster, that was built the present residence of the reigning monarch, Buckingham Palace (27), on the site of what were fields and mulberry orchards, the property of the Duke of Buckingham.

As the centre for world trade, for commerce and fashion, for theatre and pleasure, London has remained pre-eminent since she gained supremacy of the high seas in the first Elizabethan era, and gathered in the wealth of Britain's expanding empire. And though that empire is now dissolving into independent nationhood, London remains full of the fascinating architecture of those stirring centuries. Yet London was never a great centre of art (though trading in art treasures) or of learning. She had no university until recently; Oxford and Cambridge alone supplied that want for many centuries.

THE SOUTH AND EAST

In and around London lie the homes of a dozen million of her workers, of which it is said that six million commute daily in and out of the centre. Some of these are fortunate in living in the still unspoilt small villages beyond the "Green Belt" of country which at present (but for how long?) insulates the main conurbia. Others, living within London, week-end in the Home Counties and its coast (31, 39). There are the rolling South Downs (33) for walkers and riders, where the ancient flower-starred turf once quivered to the westward march of pre-Christian man, his nomad families, his herds and flocks, and presently his foes. The little South Coast harbours are today filled with the white sails of lovers of small boats using their new leisure healthfully pottering by the sea (39) or racing their class boats (37).

These home counties are worthy of a slow inquiring pilgrimage, so that the full flavour of coast and countryside scenes, interspersed with visits to historic buildings, may remain in the memory. There are cosy and comfortable inns (35, 39) of great age to linger in, and famous houses (79), castles, churches and cathedrals (29, 43) to study, and the changing architecture of the old villages in relation to local stone, or absence of stone, remarked.

Many churches and other ecclesiastical buildings still in use are of Norman foundation, a few Saxon; centuries-old monuments within attest the remembered piety (much of it death-bed, perhaps) of forefathers in quaint language, with effigies and Christian symbols on carven sepulchre and tombstone. Old yew trees hang their evergreen boughs over hoary churchyards which are often today a neglected riot of wild flowers and singing birds, delighting the searcher for peace and contemplation. But here and there God's Acre is kept as a well-tended garden.

Close by invariably lies one or more ancient alehouses (47, 73), surviving perhaps from long before the days of the regular mail-coach, and rebuilt since. Low wooden beams and mullioned windows give to inn and village house alike that reassuring atmosphere of warm antiquity loved by both native and foreigner, an atmosphere which it is now fashionable to try to recapture when building anew. Inn stables today are usually converted to garage cars, but there is often a stall available for the odd mount, a riding hack, seldom a draught horse. Riding is still popular, despite car- and lorry-congested roads. And every county has one or more packs of foxhounds or beagles which meet in the hunting season at country inn, squire's house, or cross-roads near the covert.

The inn is the meeting point for friends, or to discuss a quiet business, or love, affair. We say, "I'll be at the *Swan, Lion, Lamb, Bear, King's Arms, Star, Crown, Anchor, George . . .*" and we visualise the beamed ceiling, the blazing fire, the polished brass, inside, and the brightly-painted, gaudy, stylised sign swinging from bracket or post, outside. Some of us even "collect" the many quaint signs with camera (e.g. *Pig & Whistle, Cow & Snuffers)*, and I knew one bird lover who claimed to have listed every inn named after a bird.

The village church and inn often lie together beside the village green or common, where on fine summer evenings the inhabitants stroll or play games, as of old—though the games may be modern or modernised—especially cricket. Here, too, the annual fair takes place. In large country towns the village green has become the public square, where usually a weekly open market of booths attracts a busy crowd of shoppers to buy country produce, the wares of itinerant tradesmen, and the trash of hucksters. It was a Saxon king, Edward the Elder, who decreed that all buying and selling must take place in the market place.

Commons and common lands may stretch far into the country, with rights of grazing and turbary (protected by ancient, originally feudal, by-laws) enjoyed by local landholders. The public generally have full access, but the same by-laws usually forbid abuse (fires, litter, hunting). These public lands have never been built upon; they are remnant of the primeval "waste" of Britain, grazed, overgrazed, and often today reverted to forest. Here and there they are moderately extensive still, as the Surrey heaths, the North (Kent) Downs, the South (Sussex) Downs (33), Epping Forest in Essex, Alice Holt Forest and the New Forest (45) in Hampshire.

THE SOUTH AND WEST

The New Forest lies west of Southampton Water, where ships were built of the forest oak during centuries of sail. In spite of its name it is the oldest Royal Forest in England. The wild boar and wolves hunted by the Norman kings who named the New Forest have long since vanished, replaced by herds of ponies. But the deer are still plentiful, and managed by honorary verderers in collaboration with the Forestry Commission. This forest is alive with wild life, from rare plants and butterflies to red, fallow, and roe deer, badger and fox and buzzard. As a fresh-air lung for townsfolk it has now become almost too popular for the continued prosperity of these creatures—visitors need to be more careful about fast driving of cars, fires and litter.

After the Forest the land westwards opens upon the dry plains and broad vales of Dorset and South Wiltshire. Here was living space for the pastoral tribes who by day grazed their flocks on the chalky savannah and hunted plover and bustard and hare with slingstones, and by night withdrew to upland camps behind palisades of earth and stakes. Wolves, bears and hostile neighbours lurked in neighbouring woods.

Salisbury Plain for centuries has been the meeting place of the early inhabitants of Britain, doubtless because it could accommodate thousands of grazing animals on its wide pastures. The great circles of Stonehenge were begun by the neolithic people about 1800 B.C.

Its importance may be estimated from the fact that within a day's walk of Stonehenge there are 345 barrows or burial mounds. Also that some of the stones were transported from the Preseli Mountains of Pembrokeshire (evidently sacred to the priesthood of that time), a journey by sea and land of not less than 150 miles. If one could but glimpse the face of the architect who designed Stonehenge! The alignment of the principal stones of Stonehenge and other circles is proved to be connected with sun-worship. The line between the sun at the horizon at sunrise on the day of summer solstice (21st June) and the death of the sun at sunset on the night (21st December) of winter solstice runs through the outlying Heelstone and the centre of the Stonehenge circle. On solstice days (and probably on days marked by the Stonehenge sundial between, in the same way) the great festivals were kept, when law-giving and sacrifice to the Sun-God drew the tribal families to pay homage to the wise men, soothsayers and priests who could interpret the calendar, and foretell the future by the movement of the life-giving sun.

These pastoral and hunting neolithic and Bronze Age peoples slept at night in skin tents, like the Lapps of Scandinavia today. Where their settlements were more permanent, along the ridges of grassy hills, they built the first houses, merely excavating a hole in the ground about two feet deep, throwing the soil around and walling it inside with stones or rubble; the roof would be of skins or thatch. Traces of these "hut-circles" occur everywhere on hills and cliff-tops in Britain. At a time when Egypt had built her temples and employed goldsmiths to make exquisite tomb furnishings, the ancient Britons had not yet built a stone-tiled roof—although beehive type huts with conical roofs of overlapping stone were known, and may be seen in Wales and Ireland today; their date is uncertain, as they were also used by Christians.

It was the Romans who brought the modern art of the mason to Britain. Possibly they were the first despoilers of Stonehenge, which they would have regarded as they regarded the Druidic rites of the Celtic priests, as a threat to their authority. They occupied first the hill-top forts such as Maiden Castle, Old Sarum, Cissbury Ring, massacring all who would not submit (excavations at the entrance to the great fortress of Maiden Castle in Dorset have revealed the mutilated skeletons of men and women). With the subsequent *Pax Romana*, Roman villas, complete with baths and gymnasia, farms, mills, and huts for slaves, sprang up, built with local stone. Although the bondmen and their families still continued to live in wooden huts and wattle-and-mud hovels, freedmen began to build stone houses in villages and towns during the next three hundred years. Bath (49) with its Roman villas near the hot springs (these fully exploited) became a favourite spa in the Romano-British period.

THE MIDLANDS

Nowhere are the subtle shades of weathered local stone more pleasing in England than in the Cotswold Hills (87), where many villages and towns (91, 97) are built wholly of the soft yellow oolite limestone, with roofs carrying thick tiles of the same material, darkened with age and lichen. Fortunately the planning authority is now strict to preserve this pleasing appearance. Bath Stone (49) is a good example of the most durable type of Cotswold rock, and has been extensively used in towns and for college and cathedral.

The slate quarries of Wales produced the finest thin tough roofing slates, which were elsewhere in England in great demand in the building boom of the Victorian era, and which explains why so much of the mountain scenery in North Wales exhibits great man-made gashes in the sedimentary strata. Much of the Welsh border country has red sandstone to give warm colour to houses, walls, fields, from Brecon and Hereford north into Cheshire, until the grey Derbyshire limestone appears. This red sandstone appears in Devon too, though rabby and not good building stone. But in the far Isles of Orkney St Magnus' Cathedral in Kirkwall glows rose-red with the warm Orcadian sandstone.

The peaty low-lying alluvial soils and fens of Middle and Eastern England are without rock, like London. Thousands of tons of imported stone were used to build London, Cambridge, Ely, and other low-level cities. Much of it came from the ridge of limestone crossing the western midlands, from the Cotswolds to Yorkshire. Channel Islands granite was brought up the Thames, and magnesium limestone from Yorkshire, and even Caen stone from Normandy (29). Many Roman villas in London were built of Kentish stone. Later the fenland houses were built of brick, but at first they were made of timber-framing with cob (chopped straw mixed with clay). Many of these exist today to delight the eye (35, 51, 75, 79, 81).

Of course wood and brick are easier to handle than stone; masons began to compete with carpenters to give the brick infilling a new refinement, such as setting the brick on edge, herring-bone pattern, and also covering the façade with elaborate designs in plaster. But the carpenters had their styles too. One may notice the diversity in half-timbered buildings. Some are close-set with oaken uprights (35). Others, like the George Inn at Norton St Philip (51), and at Tewkesbury (81), have a draught-board pattern, with strong curved diagonal braces which give both rigidity and grace. Where brick infilling is covered with plaster and this moulded into local designs such as rosettes and quatrefoils, it is known as "pargetting"—as in the "Magpie" houses of the West Midlands.

EAST ANGLIA

The land of the Angles, who anciently settled the flooded country of marsh (reclaimed from the sea) and fen (reclaimed from fresh-water), is wide open to the sky, which is its charm in summer, though bitter cold in winter gales. Here the builders had the same problem of lack of stone. They became expert in making use of the white and black flint, often to create designs of great beauty in the flush-work of church and cathedral wall. Farms and cottages exhibit knapped flint and diaper brickwork of exquisite workmanship.

Centuries of unchanging peace have moulded the old towns and villages into a harmonious pattern: they seem to have grown there like beautiful old-fashioned garden flowers. It is a shock to see a newly-erected house or factory, however pleasantly designed, in the ancient landscape. It takes time to mellow our feelings about the intrusion. One may console oneself with the thought that the modern interior will doubtless be more convenient to live in, yet one has no wish to gaze long upon its exterior. As for whole new suburbs and the so-called new towns, few of us desire to go near them—yet future generations may one day find pleasure in examining the early twentieth-century garden village, much as today there is a cult which delights in Victoriana, from gas-lamp standards to Baptist chapel façades.

Although new building goes on all over eastern England and the Midlands, much of the fen country still is remote, flat, but enlivened with the towers of village churches, old wind-mills (103), tide-mills (101), forest (Thetford), sandy heaths (Brecklands), reedy broads (105). There are wonderful old houses, such as Holkham and Heveningham Halls (109), and the streets of some of the villages and old towns are indeed beautiful (113).

THE NORTH

Not all the gracious houses, mansions, palaces and religious buildings are concentrated in the prosperous south-eastern plain of England. But as that prosperity and its population increased, pioneers pushed out north and west in search of new lands to colonise, forcing deep into the rugged mountains and steep-sided vales and dales. They began to exploit the minerals: coal, iron, and limestone chiefly, and the textile trade from the sheep-flocks. Industrial towns sprang up with little regard for other than the profits of the new captains of these industries. One can now study in true perspective the effect of the blind rush of the Victorian age to exploit the coal-fed, steam-powered mill and iron and steel works before the advent of universal electric power. A comely rural village or small town suddenly became the base for industry. It was immediately surrounded by rows of mean and ugly houses in an attached line, well away from the mill- or mine-owner's park. But with land values soaring and the town now too be-grimed for a gentleman, the principal character enjoying this opulence departed, retired in all likelihood with a knighthood or baronetcy and a fine house in clean country if not also in London. Many of these industrial slums remain, though rehousing goes on apace. And the growing power of the trade unions in collective bargaining has ensured at last a fair deal for the coal-miners, the foundry workers, the factory and mill hands of Lancashire and Yorkshire, and the Tyneside shipwrights.

That is one side of the North. The other is very different. Few other industrial regions have such easy access to such a beautiful hinter-land of mountains, moors and lakes along the Pennine Chain. In the south are Dovedale and the lovely limestone hills of the Peak District, now a National Park on the doorstep of Manchester and Sheffield. To the north-west lie many lakes in the Lakeland National Park (123, 125), easy yet spectacular country for climbing and walking where Wordsworth and Ruskin climbed and walked. The Yorkshire Ridings are glorious with moors of purple heather and dales where shepherds dwell, with many a fine old church and abbey (130) to be viewed. The Cheviot Hills on the Scottish border north of the great Roman Wall provide 200 square miles of the loneliest rolling mountainside in England.

WALES

Little that we have so far written about South-ern England, but much that we have said about the North, applies to the land of Wales. We have mentioned, however, the common back-ground of neolithic occupation, during which occurred the amazing transport of the heavy bluestones from Preseli Mountain in Pem-brokeshire to Stonehenge in the second millen-ium B.C. Pembrokeshire was evidently early colonised by the seafarers from Iberia; it lay in the fairway at the entrance to the Irish Sea, and was later to receive the first Christian evangelist monks from Ireland. We have mentioned the survival of the Welsh language in the fastness of the mountains into which the Anglo-Saxons forced the British people. The Anglo-Saxons named the mountain country "Weales" which means "Foreigners"; for many centuries they feared raiding by the Welsh. A Welsh war song runs:

> *The mountain sheep are sweeter,*
> *But valley sheep are fatter;*
> *We therefore deemed it meeter*
> *To carry off the latter.*

Strangely enough (in view of their fratricidal tendencies) the Welsh knew themselves as the *Kymry*, that is, "Comrades". They would only combine to meet a common enemy, or raid the English usurpers. About 700 the Saxons felt compelled to shut the Welshmen in with the great wall of Offa's Dyke, from the River Dee to the River Severn. Owain Glyndwr was the last of the guerilla leaders to lead a united Wales against the English crown, and hold a Welsh parliament (1400–16).

The great fiord of Milford Haven, described by Nelson as one of the finest in the world, has lately come into its own; its deep water can accommodate the largest ships ever built, up to 120,000 tons, alongside the new ocean terminal wharves of international oil companies. Just outside lie the flower-decked, sea-bird, cliff-bound nature reserves of the islands of Skokholm, Grassholm, Skomer, Ramsey, and others with names bestowed by raiding Vikings who wintered their longships within Milford's waters.

But it is the mountains which have kept Wales and the Welsh people inviolate. From the Brecon Beacons north to Merioneth they are wild and little-known sheep-runs, where Welsh mountain ponies (133) graze around little lakes and reservoirs (135). The North Wales massif attracts hundreds of climbers and tourists. It is stark mountain country of eerie beauty where cool glacial lakes or *llyns* (135), treeless and rockbound, have inspired sombre legends. It is dominated by the five peaks of Snowdon (Welsh, *Eryri*, "Eagle's nest"), 3,560 feet, from which the view embraces both England and Ireland.

SCOTLAND

The scenery of Scotland is peerless in its changing beauty and grandeur; mountain, glen, loch, rushing river and white waterfall, and close on a thousand islands of the sea bemuse the visitor who travels far between Lowland and Highland. Added to these is the romantic history of the Scots people, the picturesque division into clans each with its tartan dress, and their traditional hospitality. These (to say nothing of that principal beverage and export, whisky) have brought international fame to Scotland, justly; and one of her best publicists has been the novelist Sir Walter Scott, whose memory is enshrined in the Memorial in Edinburgh (139), while his house at Abbotsford is preserved for the nation.

The Lowlands comprise approximately all the country south of the line of foothills north of the Clyde and Forth, and include the low country along the north-east coast. They were the first lands to succumb, for geographical reasons, to the invading Romans and English,

although retaining for a while a separate government under English rule. Famous Lowland clans include the Macdougalls, Gordons, Douglas, Scotts, Stewarts, Hamiltons, Cunninghams, Kennedys, Johnstones, Homes and Elliots, names today still very much on the electoral rolls of the same clan lands.

Generally more fertile and with a better climate, the Lowlands were much raided by men of the Highland clans living in the barren mountains and glens of the north. When not fighting among themselves the Highlanders made forays deep into the fat low country. A rough code of unwritten laws was respected between rival clans, and among these rules of convenience were those of hospitality, honour among thieves, respect for women and children, and freedom of movement. The last was essential to permit the passage of reavers (raiders) through the territory of another clan, which would require a toll or "collup" to be paid, and this took the form of a tithe or more of the stolen cattle and sheep.

The code was freely broken (there is a Gaelic saying, "Feed you today, fight you tomorrow", which describes the nature of their hospitality); and each detail of theft, burning and killing would be remembered, and would require a reckoning, if not by the insulted clansman, then by his children or grandchildren. The notorious Massacre of Glencoe was inspired indirectly by this sort of long-nursed hatred arising out of a tribal feud. Yet, when a general invasion threatened, the "Fiery Cross" was sent by runner from one glen to another, with a note giving the place of muster of the clans against the common enemy. Sir Walter Scott describes how the cross was carried flaming for roadless miles by loch and glen; but it is certain that it would have burned out, and in fact it is believed to have been a wooden cross with its extremities charred and dipped into the blood of a goat sacrificed at the moment of the alarm.

A map of the Highland clans and families shows that the Campbells controlled most of Argyll. The Mackenzies dominated the wild fastness of Wester Ross (161) and the Isle of Lewis, profiting from the forfeiture of the Macdonalds, who were Lords of the Isles and famous pipers. Other Hebridean clans were the Macleods of Skye (151, 159) and the Macleans of Mull. The eastern Highlands from Caithness to Stirling were parcelled out between the Sinclairs, Sutherlands, Rosses, Murrays, Macintoshs, Grants, Gordons, Stewarts, Forbes, Lindsays, Grahams, etc.

It was easier for the inhabitants of the coast, because they had the fishing to fall back upon, to survive the great clearances of the Highlands (1780-1850) which removed the overpopulated and hungry clan families in favour of the landlord's sheep. Cruel as this forced exodus was, it led to the establishment of prosperous communities with new opportunities overseas, especially in Canada, Australia and New Zealand, which so badly needed colonists at the time.

With her troubled history it might be expected that Scotland is rich in historic buildings; and this is so. They range from crude neolithic stone monuments and villages (e.g. in Orkney, Shetland, Outer Hebrides) to the exquisite abbeys of the east coast and the border country. The Office of Works and the National Trust for Scotland care for many of these; and the Trust has preserved a great variety of beautiful country as well, including a whole village, an island (Fair Isle), and part of Glencoe (155). There are National Forest Parks in Argyll (37,000 acres); the Glen More area of the Cairngorm Mountains, where you may see red deer, reindeer, ptarmigan, snow-bunting and golden eagle; and the 100 square miles of Glen Trool National Forest Park in Galloway. There are many nature reserves in Scotland, notably the Island of Rhum (eagles, shearwaters, deer); North Rona, Outer Hebrides (seals and petrels); and the 10,000 acres of the spectacular and beautiful Beinn Eighe Reserve by Loch Maree (161).

NORTHERN IRELAND

In the fourth and fifth centuries Northern Ireland, then known as Ulster, was one of five kingdoms of ancient Ireland. But as far back as 6000 B.C. the Stone Age peoples had settled there; no country in Europe may have so much evidence of neolithic occupation by the small dark race, whose magic with stone monument building possibly gave rise to the Irish legends of the goblin-like leprechauns. The Niall princes of Ulster gave up the Druidic religion in the fifth century and became ardent Christians. Their plundering raids along the Irish sea-coasts resulted in the capture of one Patrick, as a young man in west Wales, about 432. He became Bishop of Armagh, where two cathedrals are dedicated to him today; and patron saint of Ireland. It was from Ireland that the wave of Christianity swept back over Europe, through the missionary saints, of which St Columba is perhaps best known for his legendary voyage in a coracle from Ulster to the Hebridean Isle of Iona, and his founding of the cathedral there.

There has always been a close racial and physical relation between Northern Ireland and south-west Scotland. When the Normans attacked Ulster, a successful resistance was made, thanks to a steady supply of manpower from Scotland. But when not fighting an external war, the Scots-Irish clans fought internally.

Henry VIII was the first English king to assume the title of King of Ireland; Elizabeth I ordered confiscation of Catholic property and the plantation of loyal Protestants on Catholic Irish soil. There were savage scenes of repression and massacre, and deportation of Catholics as slaves to America. Ulster Protestants flourished while southern Ireland fell into decay. The long period of poverty culminated in the potato famine of 1846-7, when over 21,000 people died of starvation. The population of Ireland dropped from eight to its present four million, chiefly through emigration to England and overseas.

The painful period of regeneration of Ireland has ended in the present revival of the Gaelic language in Eire, and the prosperity of Northern Ireland, which is still staunchly Scots-Irish. In the peace which has come to Ireland the visitor will enjoy the freedom of a thinly-inhabited land all the more for its spaciousness and lack of modern pressures, the ever-ready hospitality of its cheerful peoples, and for the marvellous scenery of its coasts, loughs and mountains.

St Paul's Cathedral

The first cathedral is attributed to Ethelbert, king of Kent, about the year 604. It was destroyed by fire in 1087. During the slow rebuilding it was damaged by fire in 1136, enlarged in 1230 and 1256, a tall spire was added in 1315, and a chapter house in 1332. In the sixteenth century it became neglected, and was even used as a money-maker's meeting place. In 1666 it was severely burnt in the Great Fire of London.

Christopher Wren received his knighthood in 1674 as the result of the King's approval of his bold plan to rebuild the cathedral with a dome, an *idée fixe* of Wren's resisted by his critics until he reluctantly compromised by adding a top-heavy spire. The result is much beloved if not altogether admired by Londoners today, for it miraculously survived the heavy bombing which laid so much of the City waste during the war—one delayed-action bomb which fell beside the cathedral fortunately never exploded! Through those dark days the Dome and Cross of the City Cathedral stood proudly over surroundings lit by raging fires, a symbol of the faith of Christendom which triumphs over evil.

Photograph by A. F. Kersting

Trooping the Colour

Trooping the Colour is a ceremony mounted annually on the "official" birthday of the Sovereign in June, in which month the weather is likely to be fine and the brilliant colours of the uniforms of the Guards to be seen to best advantage. Today's pageantry doubtless originated in the annual inspection parade of the Sovereign's own soldiers, but today it is witnessed by thousands of sightseers. Usually the Queen, mounted, is attired in the uniform of the Guards regiment whose colours are being "trooped", as she reviews her Household Guards, both horse and foot, in the full splendour of their ceremonial dress.

Photograph by Colour Library International

Westminster Abbey

The first and second churches are lost, but fragments of the Norman monastery survive. The present structure was begun by Henry III who, brought up in France, followed the design of Reims Cathedral, as is clear from the great height (103 feet inside) in relation to width, the radiating circular chapels, and the polygonal apse. The name of his mason was significantly *Henry of Reyns*. After numerous set-backs, especially fires, it was completed during the fourteenth century, except for Henry VII's chapel (1503-12). The towers were added in the eighteenth century.

While all the remaining English abbeys were destroyed during the Reformation, Westminster remained intact. It was close under the control of the king and parliament. It was the burial place of monarchs and many other famous men, from Edward the Confessor (died 1066) to the present century. The oak Coronation Chair was made in 1300-1 specially to hold the Stone of Scone of Scottish kings. The vast number of memorials almost obscure the original fourteenth-century spaciousness of this Norman, gracious interior.

Photograph by A. F. Kersting

River Thames and Houses of Parliament

From the Victoria Tower we see "our Palace of Westminster" which contains the Houses of Lords and Commons. It was formerly the main residence of the King, who moved from Winchester before the Norman Conquest. William Rufus built the main Hall. The Palace was burnt down in the several fires which devoured London at intervals during the age of timber and thatch roofs. In the fire of 1834 the Palace was burnt to the ground, but the ancient Hall survived. The new Houses of Parliament were built in the Gothic style by Barry and Pugin, who won the competition for the most acceptable design. The towers were completed in 1858-60. The stone is magnesium limestone from Yorkshire. The Houses were badly damaged by German air attacks, but were completely restored.

The tidal Thames washes the terraces below; its barge-lined shores lie peacefully in the sun. But the river and the Palace of Westminster have seen stirring and disturbing events in a history of centuries of sea-adventures by men of the maritime British nation.

Photograph by British Travel and Holidays Association

Big Ben and Parliament Square

The great clock of Big Ben was completed in 1858, and for over a hundred years has announced the hours from the great tower of the Mother of all Parliaments (as the Westminster Palace is fondly called). The sound of Big Ben is broadcast daily all over the world. A wood-pigeon sits on the head of Epstein's statue of the South African, General Jan Smuts, champion of liberty (and incidentally a lover of birds). The magic hour of five approaches, when thousands of Londoners will begin to abandon town offices and the government departments in White-hall (to the left). But if the Commons are sitting the members may not rise until midnight. Big Ben will then be illuminated, and Parliament Square Gardens empty. The Gothic façade of the Houses of Parliament is one of great beauty, and has a symmetry which gives an appropriate air of elegance and dignity to a centre for the making of the law.

Photograph by Kenneth Scowen

Buckingham Palace

The Duke of Buckingham in 1705 built himself a huge red-bricked "country house" on this site. It was used by royalty from 1762, and known at that time as Buckingham House. Nearby is St James's Palace (c. 1532–1676), the former main royal court and residence. George IV began the present Buckingham Palace on the site of Buckingham's house. John Nash was the architect. It was to be commodious, to accommodate a large family and the business of the Monarch of an Empire, yet was to have extensive country-type gardens. The State Apartments are impressive; they include the Grand Hall, Throne Room, Ballroom, Music-Room, Picture Gallery, and Green, White and Blue Drawing-Rooms.

It was completed in 1847, and Queen Victoria moved in at the height of the Empire's heyday, when Britannia truly ruled the waves. In the extensive gardens, with their lawns and lake, hundreds of guests are received at the Queen's summer garden parties. The Royal Standard flies at the masthead when Her Majesty is in residence.

Photograph by A. F. Kersting

Canterbury Cathedral

Bede the historian says that the first cathedral was consecrated on the site of a Romano-British church about 602 by Augustine. It was despoiled and burnt by waves of pagan invaders and by fire. After the Norman Conquest, Lanfranc, Abbot of Caen, was appointed archbishop in 1070, and rebuilt it in seven years. On 29th December 1170 Thomas Beckett, appointed archbishop by Henry II, whose friend and Chancellor he had been, but whom he now defied as a servant no longer of King but of Pope, was slain by four of Henry's knights inside the cathedral. The foul deed resulted in Thomas's beatification three years later, and so arose the cult of St Thomas the Martyr. Thousands of pilgrims thronged Canterbury for 300 years "the holy blissful martyr for to see", as Chaucer says. Indeed the word "canter" derives from the pace of mounted pilgrims to Canterbury.

Much of the cathedral was burned in the fire of 1174. The renowned William of Sens began the rebuilding; when he fell from the scaffolding, another genius of the name of William ("the English") carried on. The stone was brought from Caen by sea and river to within three miles of the cathedral.

Photograph by British Travel and Holidays Association

Beachy Head, Sussex

Although the new Lighthouse does rest on the chalk beach under the Head, the word "Beachy" is a corruption of *Beau-chef*, the "beautiful headland". The first lighthouse was known as Belle-Tout, westwards along the cliff; but as these 500 feet high walls of chalk are forever crumbling into the sea and often wrapped in mist, it was replaced by the present conspicuously painted structure at sea-level. There were beacons here in medieval, if not Roman, times, now fallen seawards. The friable rock, totally unstable to the human climber, safely houses nesting gulls and peregrine falcons; the latter were much prized by English kings for hawking.

It is possible to get down to the sea near here, at Birling Gap. Nearer Eastbourne there is an inn and a Coastguard look-out on the cliff lane.

Photograph by Noel Habgood

The South Downs, Sussex

The South Downs are a range of undulating chalk hills stretching west from Eastbourne and swinging somewhat inland above Chichester, and towards Winchester. It is possible to walk from one end to another on the springy flower-starred turf, except that one must descend to cross three little rivers which force their way towards the sea: Cuckmere, Ouse and Adur. Views are magnificent from beacon to beacon, and hill-top to beechen ring. At one time the Downs were cultivated before the valleys were deforested. Cissbury Ring was inhabited by neolithic, Roman and Saxon peoples. Sheep have made a profitable investment for centuries of Sussex farmers, but lately the plough has returned to cultivate for barley—the "bere" of ox-plough days.

The picture is taken from the north slopes of Firle Beacon (718 feet) looking towards Glynde—famed for its summer music festival today.

Photograph by Noel Habgood

The Star Inn, Alfriston, Sussex

Alfriston lies in the sleepy valley of the tiny Cuckmere River. The remains of its market cross and its large fourteenth-century church prove that it was formerly an important trading town. Records inform us that it once had a racecourse, and went in for smuggling, and throve on sales of downland sheep. There is a well-preserved thatched and timbered Priest's House close to the dignified, spired church on the common. The Star Inn is very old, yet very comfortable; its heavily timbered walls date from the late fifteenth century. It was at that time a hostel for mendicant friars and refuges. Today it houses happy honeymoon couples and other fortunate visitors who come to enjoy its serene and beautiful situation in the fold of the downs.

Photograph by A. C. K. Ware (Trust Houses Ltd)

34

Racing on the Solent

The Solent was once a river flowing eastwards from the hills of the Devon peninsula. The tides still have a strong eastwards flow before Atlantic winds which roar up past the Needles, over the shallows between Hurst Castle and Yarmouth at Solent's western entrance. Tides and tricky winds make sailing exciting. If the amateur yachtsman is not to get into difficulties, if he is to win his race, a knowledge of these changing conditions and how to use them is vital.

Cowes at the northern point of the Isle of Wight faces the wide entrance to Southampton Water, and is the world's most famous yachting centre. Many classic annual sailing races start or end here, from round-island events to transocean crossings.

Photograph by Beken & Son, Ltd

The Crown and Anchor, Dell Quay, Sussex

Dell Quay comes into the area recently designated for special protection as of outstanding natural beauty. The Crown and Anchor is a restoration of the original sixteenth-century inn. This delightful backwater of Chichester Harbour is still open to small cargo boats at high tide, although now the resort of the ever-growing fraternity of small-boat sailors which augment the local fishermen. The huge, flat, wild, marshy peninsula of Selsey to the south is a world of wildfowl, fishermen and fresh air. Here the Saxon Aella and his sons landed about 478. One of the sons was Cissa, after whom Chichester is named. The long shingle beaches are rich in fossils, and many Roman and other coins have been unearthed by the ever-eastwards-drifting pebbles. Coast erosion is said to have swallowed up an earlier cathedral and monastery built by Wilfrid of York, who landed here in 681 from Northumbria.

The 277 feet spire of Chichester's present cathedral lies safe inland to the north.

Photograph by Kenneth Scowen

Ewhurst, Surrey

This picturesque village demands exploration. It has an interesting church, with one of the finest Norman doorways in Britain (about 1140); the central tower is a 1838 "Norman" reconstruction, by Ebbels. Like so many Surrey villages Ewhurst is becoming packed with new houses along its disjointed main street and side-lanes; but exteriorly these conform generally to the nineteenth-century pattern of brick. Earlier cottages are half-timbered, with brick infilling. Time can be spent profitably examining the craftsmanship displayed in their construction, and of that of some larger country houses of the same age in the district. A Roman road marches from Farley Heath to Rowhook through pleasant lanes. There are very good inns, and a common.

Photograph by Kenneth Scowen

Salisbury Cathedral

The present cathedral stands within a green lawn setting which is possibly the most beautiful in the world, with ancient houses around, and a bishop's palace begun in 1220. But the first cathedral was begun in 1092 in a windy sterile spot on the defensive site of Old Sarum, an Iron Age fort $1\frac{1}{4}$ miles out of New Sarum (Salisbury). The Pope's permission was granted in 1200 to remove to the valley which Henry of Avranches declared at that time to be full of lilies, roses, violets, nightingales and corn, a place "fitter for exiled Adam even than his Paradise of Eden". Sixty years went into the completion, and forty more in additions. The famous spire was heightened in 1334; it is now 404 feet. The cathedral is built of the local mellow Chilford stone; and is beautifully proportioned, the square tower with its octagonal spire rising from the exact centre. Purbeck marble lends its solid elegance to the shafted windows and doorways.

Photograph by A. F. Kersting

In the New Forest, Hampshire

In order to indulge his love of hunting William the Conqueror declared a large area west of Southampton Water as his "New Forest". Early historians claim that to do this he "laid waste thirty miles of fertile land with thirty-six churches and villages". But Cobbett (1826) scornfully points out that the most fertile of lands could not have supported such a huge population, and that this area has always been poor, barren heath—a view with which geologists have since agreed. The forest laws of Canute, and after him the Norman kings, were severe in order to control the vert (timber) and venison (red, fallow and roe deer) and wild boar. These laws have been modified down the centuries and are administered by a court of verderers or Swainmote, meeting at Lyndhurst. Deer, ponies and gypsies are still very much at home in the plantations and heaths of this ancient forest.

The Rufus Stone marks the spot where William II was accidentally killed by an arrow when hunting in August 1100.

Photograph by J. Allan Cash

44

The Langton Arms, Tarrant Monkton, Dorset

Narrow country lanes wind across the lovely downland of Cranborne Chase from Shaftesbury to Poole, through quiet villages which have from time immemorial served the farmers and shepherds of these chalky uplands. There are many Romano-British "native" settlements here, notably Hinton Martell, and at Ashmore, where the village centres around a large prehistoric dewpond. There are six Tarrant villages: Tarrants Gunville, Hinton, Monkton, Rawston, Rushton and Keynston, strung along the white lane from Gunville south to Keynston, each as beautiful as the brick, thatch and cob village of this picture.

Photograph by Kenneth Scowen

FIDE ET FORTITUDINE

St James's Square, Bath

These mellow houses belong to a period when Bath was the fashionable health centre for the whole of England. Following the visit of Queen Anne in 1702 and 1703, Beau Nash became Master of Ceremonies and promoted rules of social etiquette designed to attract the rich aristocracy and their families to live in elegance in beautiful houses around the Pump Room and Assembly House. He was abetted in this by postmaster Ralph Allen, who with a keen eye to profit had bought the Combe Down quarries and produced the famous cream Bath stone; and by John Wood the architect, who used it in planning a new Bath with a Royal Forum, a Grand Circus, and terraces, parades, and crescents. Other architects flocked to beautiful Bath. John Palmer (1789-93) was responsible for Lansdown Crescent and St James's Square.

The "Hot Well" of Bath has attracted sufferers from rheumatism and arthritis since the Romans made and lined with lead the great bath. This can be seen today. The springs remain unfailingly warm at 120 degrees Fahrenheit.

Photograph by A. F. Kersting

The George Inn, Norton St Philip, Somerset

The attractive village of Norton St Philip at the cross roads from Bath to Frome enjoyed a cloth fair in medieval times. Buyers and merchants would put up at the commodious George Inn, established about 1397 for the Carthusian monks (of the priory of Hinton Charterhouse a few miles away) who enjoyed the revenue from the considerable tolls of Norton Fair. The priory is now a mere fragment; it is said that Norton's rather odd-looking church was rebuilt by a rich Norton man, Jeffrey Flower, from the choicer stones of the monastic ruins. Sir Gilbert Scott perhaps over-restored the church in 1847.

The George Inn claims the distinction of being the oldest licensed inn in England.

Photograph by British Travel and Holidays Association

Woody Bay, North Devon

Woody Bay lies west of Lynton and east of Martinhoe on the precipitous and most northern coast of Devon. Babbling Exmoor brooks force their way through steep wooded coombes, affording the only access to tiny beaches under the shadowed cliffs. When in high spate these moorland streams may flood the clinging hamlets, as happened in August 1952 when 28 bridges were swept away, and 93 houses destroyed, with 31 people drowned, at Lynmouth. The shore line rises and falls in tremendous hog-backed ridges, up to 1,000 feet high; on one of them, the Beacon, near Martinhoe, the Romans may have had a signal station to receive intelligence of any ships in the Bristol Channel approaching their Somerset settlements of towns and villas.

Photograph by J. Allan Cash

52

Hoops Inn, Horns Cross, North Devon

It is pleasant to learn that expert thatching such as this roof on the charmingly reconstructed Devon inn is still carried out; and to know that there is a Guild of Thatchers in this county—the Devon Thatchers's Association. Golden wheat straw is most often used, since ryestraw is seldom obtainable today. Reed straw is said to last longer than the twenty-five years which is reckoned to be the normal weatherproof life of "wheaten straw, the poor man's roof". Reed is sometimes used, from Somerset fens. If protected from nesting sparrows by fine mesh netting, thatch will last longer.

In some districts, where building stone is scarce, thatch, with its wide eaves, was used because it protected walls of "cob" (clay and chopped straw, mixed and applied wet) laid above a foundation of rubble and plastered over. Cob became as hard as brick when dry.

Photograph by Kenneth Scowen

Near Kingsbridge, Devon

The shallow salt river winds through peaceful farmlands from Kingsbridge south to Salcombe, affording safe mooring in quiet creeks such as this. As the tide flows, mullet, bass, flounder, mackerel and many another sea-fish feed upstream, and provide sport for both professional and amateur fishermen. The estuary is ideal for those who like to potter about in small boats. On calm days one can sail down past Salcombe into the English Channel, in sight of the lighthouse on Start Point.

Kingsbridge's granite-pillared arcade of the Shambles (1585), and St Edmund's church with its thirteenth-century tower, are beautiful. Even more lovely is Salcombe, under its sheltering western hill.

Photograph by Reece Winstone

56

Mevagissey, Cornwall

This picturesque village lies in the shelter of east-facing Mevagissey Bay, protected from prevalent westerly gales. Fishermen's houses gaze warmly down upon the inner harbour where the catch—lobsters, crabs, crayfish, pilchards, mackerel and other fish in season—is landed. Considering the popularity of the Cornish coast Mevagissey is not spoilt, but has retained a healthy independence as a small fishing port. The houses are characteristic "utilitarian Celtic" but many are redeemed by colour wash—and more ought to be. Cornish people like to attend chapels, but there is the quaint little church of Saints Meva and Ida, built of local stone, which has inside it a Norman font and a fascinating monument to Mr and Mrs Hill (1617): "Stock Lancashier, Birth London, Cornwall gave to Otwell Hill Inhabitance & Grave, Franck, Frougall, Plaisannt, Sober, Stout & Kinde"—in fact, all the seventeenth-century virtues!

Photograph by Kenneth Scowen

St Mawes, Cornwall

Not without justification the people of St Mawes claim that their climate is Mediterranean. The Atlantic, bathing the peninsulas of the Fal estuaries, drives away frost and permits palms and tender flowering shrubs to flourish. The inlet is a yachtsman's dream of a safe landlocked anchorage within a few miles of the open sea. On the north side of the creek, St Mawes faces south to the equally "sub-tropical" St Anthony-in-Roseland. Henry VIII, fearing attack from France, built (1540-3) one of his south coast castles at St Mawes Point, commanding the approach to Falmouth Harbour; it is handsomely decorated with coats of arms and gargoyles in the Renaissance style, and has a pleasing trefoil pattern of three defensive lobes.

Photograph by J. Allan Cash

Bedruthan Steps, Cornwall

On the north coast of Cornwall, Bedruthan Steps is one of many fine sandy bathing and surfing beaches facing the open Atlantic, and backed by steep cliffs where sea-birds nest and which in summer are starred with sea-pinks, campions, marigolds and vernal squill. Seals haunt the headland caves and outlying rocks. Little islets of sundered cliff stand up in sand and sea. One is called Diggory's Island, another Carnewas Island. The Cow and Calf lie just off Park Head, above which are prehistoric tumuli. A mile inland St Eval (church of St Uvelus) on the high plateau stands starkly at the edge of St Mawgan airfield. Its tall tower is a sea-mark, rebuilt by Bristol traders in 1724.

The steep descent by the Steps can be dangerous in wet weather and after cliff subsidence, and, when I last visited it, it was closed.

Photograph by Noel Habgood

62

Magdalen Tower, Oxford

The very beautiful Great Tower of Magdalen College was built in 1492. It is 144 feet high. On May morning it is customary to sing a hymn from the roof. The College and the lovely Magdalen Bridge stand at the southern entrance to the City of Oxford. The bridge is the work of John Gwynne, 1772, in the solid, practical, but handsome style that has supported well the enormous load of modern traffic it carries daily. To the left, out of the picture, is the Botanic Garden, and the beautiful Walks beside the Cherwell. One is called Addison's Walk. Addison, Hampden and Wolsey are numbered among many famous Magdalen men.

Photograph by A. F. Kersting

Compton Wynyates, Warwickshire

Compton Wynyates, the home of the Marquess of Northampton, lies in peaceful Cotswold country west of Banbury. The name has been freely translated as the hamlet or manor (*ton*) in the valley (*combe* or *cwm*) of Windgates. The Compton family were lords of the manor as far back as 1204, although the present house was not begun until the fifteenth century. Henry VIII and Elizabeth I slept there. In the Civil War the Parliamentarians attacked and partly destroyed the house after a bloody battle in 1644. It remained in disrepair until restored in the nineteenth century, when some Gothic-style "improvements" were made and the present staircase built. There are many fine portraits and pictures in the house.

Photograph by Noel Habgood

Sutton Courtenay Village, Berkshire

Another Thames-side village of great charm, with very old thatched cottages and tiled roofs, an inn, venerable chestnut and other trees, a greensward edge, and a village green on which stands the simple and solid Norman church. Opposite the church is Norman Hall, dating from 1200. The village also contains the Abbey (an infirmary for medieval monks), the Tudor Manor House of the Courtenays, and, close to the river, is "The Wharf", where Lord Oxford and Asquith lived. He was Prime Minister 1908–16, and is buried in the churchyard. The church interior is twelfth to fourteenth century and contains some interesting paintings.

Photograph by Noel Habgood

The Dining Room, Woburn Abbey, Bedfordshire

Woburn Abbey is built on the site of a Cistercian House founded by Hugh de Bolebec, 1145. John, first Earl of Bedford, Lord Privy Seal, received it (after the Abbot had been hanged from a tree for treasonable remarks against Anne Boleyn) as executor of Henry VIII's will. The Abbey as it is today is largely the work of Thomas More and Henry Flitcroft, from whose designs it was rebuilt about 1746.

The State Dining-Room is full of rare and lovely furnishings. Above the chimneypiece is the portrait of Aubert Lemire by Van Dyck, and to the right that of Queen Henrietta Maria. The dining-table is laden with Sèvres dinner service (1770), early nineteenth-century Stourbridge glass, Louis XV and XVI silver, and the famous Ascot Gold Cup (1846) (This depicts the underkeeper John Selwyn who leaped from his horse on to the back of a stag, guided it with drawn sword towards the Queen, then killed it before her!).

The grounds of Woburn have one of the finest of zoological collections, including the rare, once nearly extinct, Père David's deer from a Chinese Palace garden.

Photograph by A. F. Kersting

The Bell, Stilton, Huntingdonshire

Stilton is the headquarters of the famous cheese, where the market for the collection and sale of the commodity was established by farmers far back in medieval history. Originating in the dairies of the rolling lowlands and flat fens of Huntingdonshire, the recipe has spread over the world, and it is now no longer exclusively a Stilton village product. The handsome Bell Inn has a seventeenth-century provenance. The village church is Early English, with Perpendicular additions, and contains interesting memorials. Ermine Street, a Roman road, runs due north-south through Stilton on this main highway of A1.

Photograph by British Travel and Holidays Association

Lacock Village, Wiltshire

Half-timbered gabled houses arrest the traveller with their peaceful beauty in this venerable village. The doorway of the Angel Inn is sixteenth century. In East Street is a fine Lockup and fourteenth-century barn. Well worth a visit is Lacock Abbey, now a National Trust property, still occupied, a gracious religious house which was converted to secular use after the suppression of the monasteries. When Henry VIII's Commissioners visited the Abbey they found the nuns "afforded to the town and all other adjoining by common report a great relief"; even the accounts were in perfect order; and for five years more the nuns had grace to continue, with pensions granted on surrender of the Abbey in 1539. It was bought by Sir William Sherington from the King, and it is Sir William's Tudor work that gives delight today to this house founded in 1229 in a meadow then known as Snaylesmede.

Photograph by H. J. Stapleton

Shakespeare Memorial Theatre, Stratford-upon-Avon

The present Memorial Theatre was built in 1932; the architect was Elizabeth Whitworth Scott. It has settled well into its beautiful riverine background, although it was at first the subject of a fierce dispute over its style. It replaces an earlier theatre burnt down in 1926. Shakespeare's plays never cease to attract thousands to the "Season" at Stratford, which has recently had to be extended because of this tremendous demand for seats at the Memorial Theatre performances.

A William Shakespeare, and also a Christopher Marlowe, were born in 1564, and controversy still is heard as to who wrote the Shakespeare plays. Or was Bacon the author? What really matters is that there existed an Englishman of extraordinary genius who could write such immortal blank verse and sonnets.

Photograph by Noel Habgood

Anne Hathaway's Cottage, Shottery

Shottery lies a mile west of Stratford-upon-Avon. The thatched and timbered cottage is the birthplace of Anne Hathaway, wife of one "Wm. Shakespeare". We know little about the life of the dramatist, or of his wife. In his will this Shakespeare does not mention his work as an author, or that he wrote or owned a single play. A William Shakespeare is buried in Holy Trinity Church, Stratford, which contains his monument, the font in which he was christened, and the register of his baptism and burial. Stratford is a lovely old town where one may see these things, and gaze at the old houses, the Grammar School, church, streets, and other landmarks known to the genius of the English Renaissance.

Anne's cottage can be reached by a pleasant footpath walk from the town.

Photograph by Kenneth Scowen

Tewkesbury Abbey and River, Gloucestershire

The waters of the Avon mingle with the broader Severn near the old mill at Tewkesbury. This rural town has a number of timber-framed houses dating back to the sixteenth century, and some with projecting upper storeys that may be older. The river provides boating and coarse fishing.

   The 148-feet-high tower of the Abbey dominates the ancient town. It was built on the site of a Saxon monastery. Feudal Normans found wealth in Tewkesbury from Cotswold wool and Severn cornfields, and they rebuilt the Benedictine church by 1150; but it was ruined by fire in 1178, then rebuilt and enlarged for the next 200 years. On 4th May 1471 the Battle of Tewkesbury was fought between the roses of York and Lancaster; Queen Margaret of Anjou was utterly defeated and her son Prince Edward put to death.

Photograph by Kenneth Scowen

80

The Crypt, Worcester Cathedral

Of all the crypts of its date that of Worcester Cathedral must be the most beautiful. The arrangement of the arches resting on a central pillar was unique, though much copied since. There was at first a wooden church, probably erected by Christian Celts before they were defeated by English pagans in 577. After the Danes sacked the monastery in 1041, Wulfstan was elected Bishop. Because of his piety and personality he was the sole English bishop to remain when the Normans conquered England; as a result he was venerated, and in due course canonised, and his enshrined relics became sacred to avert eternal damnation. King John, his sins evidently heavy upon him, left orders for his burial beside the shrine of St Wulfstan and his predecessor St Oswald (of the first church). The crypt was built in 1029.

Photograph by A. F. Kersting

82

The Wye at Symond's Yat, Monmouth

At Symond's Yat there are glorious views towards the foothills of Wales. Here the Welsh-born River Wye flows first north, then westwards, and finally southwards to make almost a complete circle as it seeks to escape between the cliffs rising 500 feet above the verdant valley. Southwards is the enchanting Forest of Dean, a very interesting old woodland of great extent, where sheep and deer mingle with coal mines and conifers, and where you nevertheless can walk for miles without meeting a human soul. The Wye is famous for its salmon and trout fishing, and there are boats to be hired. The ancient walled town of Monmouth is an ideal centre for exploring a little-known countryside of much beauty; and nearby is famed Tintern Abbey.

Photograph by J. Allan Cash

View looking west from Cotswold ridge

The true Cotswold Hills lie on a north-east south-west line within the county of Gloucester. They rise almost to one thousand feet, gently on the south-east side, abruptly from the fertile Severn Plain on the north-west. This northern escarpment looks down on the bustling city of Gloucester and the more leisurely spa of Cheltenham. Here and there are wide views of the distant Malverns, the Forest of Dean, the Wye Valley, Herefordshire and the eastern spurs of the Welsh mountains. Cotswold economy has been based on the "golden hoof" of sheep, without which the thin soil would have grown thinner; but these lower slopes are more fertile and suitable for cattle.

Photograph by J. Allan Cash

A Cotswold Farm

The oolitic limestone outcrops plentifully in the Cotswold Hills. It is easily split into flat slabs, primrose yellow when first exposed, darkening and growing hoary with weather and lichen. All the farms and the field-walls are built of this stone, and often the roofs are tiled with it, finely split. This uniformity is most satisfying.

The soil is not rich, but from Roman times onwards there is evidence that great flocks of sheep grazed these hills—the Roman villa at Chedworth had a wool-fulling mill. The nuns of Holy Trinity Abbey at Caen in Normandy owned 1,700 sheep on Minchinhampton Down. Cotswold place-names remind us of the success of the sheep which throve so well on the dry slopes free of footrot and fluke of the low ground; e.g. Sheepscombe, and the numerous Shiptons, and Shipston.

Photograph by A. F. Kersting

Broadway, Worcestershire

Broadway Village High Street, lined with green grass, is one of the showpieces of traditional Cotswold country, built as it is exclusively of the oolitic limestone, and old into the bargain. Many houses are beautiful examples of mellow sixteenth-century work. The parish church of St Eadburgh is older still, a perfect gem as it stands by the stream some distance from the village through which the main road traffic streams so tirelessly. The little church seems to be brooding peacefully over its Norman and Early English days, under the Down which rises nearly a thousand feet above sea-level. Five hundred feet up on top of the steep hill above Broadway itself stands Broadway Monument, a hefty tower or folly built in 1800 in pseudo-medieval style by the Earl of Coventry, prideful landowner, so that he might see the glorious view over the land in his possession.

Photograph by John Tarlton

Castle Combe, Wiltshire

So-called because of the now-ruined Castle on the hill above the valley or "coomb". The ancient timber-roofed cross is the centre of this hamlet on the borders of Gloucestershire and Wiltshire; around it lie the church, the manor house (1664-1873), inn, post-office, antique shop, and colour-washed houses roofed with moss-grown local tiles. The whole is bowered in trees, an utterly peaceful scene, although apt to be crowded on high days and holidays with admiring visitors.

St Andrew's Church has a very fine chancel arch in the French late thirteenth-century style, and a magnificent tower with buttresses and fan-vault, begun in 1434. The bell-turret of the demolished church at Biddlestone, a nearby village, has been reassembled in the grounds of the Manor House.

Photograph by Kenneth Scowen

Bourton-on-the-Water, Gloucestershire

A sizeable village of utopian beauty. The clear waters of the Windrush, glittering with star-wort and water plants, invite the visitor to stand and stare. He will see fine trout swimming in this stream which rises a few miles away in the Cotswold Hills. The bridges are elegant, the streets broad, and the trees charmingly arranged. It is an ideal centre for exploring the neighbourhood, remarkable for its many-worded place-names, including the Upper and Lower Swells and Slaughters:

> *Bourton-on-the-Water's*
> *Close to both the Slaughters;*
> *Stow-on-the-wold as well's*
> *Next door to both the Swells.*
> *But Bourton-on-the-Hill*
> *Is far and lonely still.*

Each has its church, of Norman origin, and the locality is full of the evidence of megalithic and Roman occupation.

Photograph by Kenneth Scowen

Snowshill, Gloucestershire

High up on the Cotswold Hills, Snowshill is a remote and very beautiful hamlet off the beaten track. Cottage and Church are of the warm native limestone, including the heavy tiles on the roofs of both. Favourite old English garden flowers give a summer air to the wide exposed country over which fierce winter gales and snow may blow. The views are grand towards Bredon Hill in Worcestershire, on the boundary of which county Snowshill lies. The little church of St Barnabas was rebuilt one hundred years ago.

Photograph by Kenneth Scowen

96

Landscape, Terling, Essex

This peaceful, early summer scene along warm, tree-lined lanes where hedge-parsley "whitely greets the wandering lovers" is typical of the rolling inland Essex country, little known although so close to London. Visitors who seek for quietude are delighted with the feeling of remoteness of so much of this country of endless variety, which begins southwards in the suburbs of London, and ends northwards in the meandering beauties of the River Stour.

Pretty Terling village has the immemorial air of its long history of farming days. The church has a 1732 west tower with handsome arched doorway and windows; and there is a seventeenth-century Friends Meeting House where Quakers formerly held their simple services; and a smock mill.

Photograph by John Tarlton

98

Woodbridge Mill, Suffolk

In country barely above sea-level the water-mill was perforce worked by the movement of the tide—one or both ways. A tide-mill existed at Woodbridge in Norman times (1170). But now few or none are at work—this one recently broke its main oaken shaft. The ancient timber-framed structure is protected by corrugated iron sheeting beneath its picturesque mansard roof of tiles.

Usually wind power worked the mills of East Anglia, and there are still two to be seen near Woodbridge: the old tower mill known as Tricker's, now derelict; and Buttram's Mill, built in 1816 and sixty feet high, a conspicuous landmark. The last had four patent sails, and although now not working, it is fortunately kept in repair by the County Council.

Photograph by Hallam Ashley

Paston Mill, Norfolk

There are still windmills to be seen in East Anglia, but few are now working, thanks to the development of more reliable engines independent of the airs of heaven. The broken mill and wind-blown corn stooks attest the breezes of the coast close to which Paston stands. In the fourteenth-century church are monuments of the Paston family, whose letters have told us much about the way of life in the Middle Ages. Marriages then were "arranged" and dowries bargained for, and children begot annually. When young Elizabeth objected to marrying an ugly fifty-year-old widower she was beaten black and blue by her mother daily until she gave in. But at least one love-at-first-sight Paston match succeeded, it is pleasant to find, because the mother was "soft-hearted".

Photograph by Hallam Ashley

The Pleasure Boat, Hickling, Norfolk

The slow-moving rivers of East Anglia twist and turn over the flat landscape, forming the shallow lakes known as the Broads. These lie mainly north-west of Great Yarmouth, into whose tidal basin the main navigable drain, the River Bure, empties. Hickling Broad is one of the largest of these lakes, and visited by many sail- and motor-boats. A holiday on the reed-fronted Broads, under the huge wide sky, is a soothing experience. There is no hurry, one can watch the swans and water-birds, hear nightingales and reed-warblers in the thickets, and study the activities of reed-cutters and fen farmers; and there is always some ancient inn at hand, like The Pleasure Boat, for a call at an appropriate hour.

Photograph by G. Douglas Bolton

Ely Cathedral, Cambridgeshire

The "Minister aet Elige" was begun in 673 by St Etheldreda. The Danes sacked it in 870. It was reconsecrated in 970. Abbot Simeon Walkelin began the present building in 1083, and the relics of Etheldreda were translated in 1106. Building was not complete before 1252. In 1322 the tower suddenly collapsed, causing great damage. A new larger octagonal tower was designed by the monk, goldsmith and sacristan, Alan of Walsingham; its soaring arches and shafts are pure delight, and the whole octagon is radiant with light from the large clerestory windows.

    The cathedral is built of oolitic limestone from Rutland quarries; the timber comes from Hertfordshire, where the monks of Ely owned forests. It stands majestically upon a little island some sixty feet above the level of the surrounding fen.

Photograph by A. F. Kersting

Interior, Heveningham Hall, Suffolk

The interior decoration of Heveningham Hall was the design of James Wyatt, a remarkable young man of classical tastes who decorated in the style of Robert Adam. The Hall was built about 1780 for a wealthy merchant of Dutch extraction on a plan prepared by Sir Robert Taylor. The picture shows what is now known as Wyatt's Hall. Warm-coloured marble columns and pilasters and the delightful cool fan vaulting give beauty and colour and firmness to the tunnel vault with its classical *paterae* and half-*paterae*. Wyatt's enthusiasm, which earned him the name of "The Destroyer" when he was on a reconstruction job, is faultless here.

Photograph by A. F. Kersting

King's College Chapel, Cambridge

The present superb Chapel was begun in 1446 but not completed until 1515. Building stone is non-existent in this Fen country; white limestone was imported from Yorkshire, but the chapel was finished in buff limestone from Weldon. Contracts naming the master-masons are extant. It has an awe-inspiring beauty and is the finest of the medieval buildings in English colleges. Height and light from the tall mullioned windows give the interior a clear and noble perspective.

The restrained classical-style house on the right is Fellows' Building, originally intended to be a grand Baroque Academic Forum by Sir Christopher Wren's secretary, who was the first architect. The Provost objecting, the plan was set aside for ten years, then James Gibbs in 1723 designed and built the present version in Portland stone. On the left we glimpse part of Clare College, which was rebuilt 1638–1715.

Photograph by Kenneth Scowen

A Street in King's Lynn, Norfolk

In the centuries of sailing ships King's Lynn on the Wash was a sea-port of considerable traffic with other North Sea towns. Sailing barges passed up the Ouse and far into the interior of England along the Bedford River and the network of canals and drains of the Isle of Ely. There is still some sea-commerce at the wharves and warehouses of the quay. The Stuart Customs House looks as important as ever beside the bridge over salt water. The narrow streets and ancient gabled houses seem to speak of those busy bygone days of maritime importance. Many fishing and pleasure boats now sail upon the tide at the flood. There is a splendid market square, guildhall, and two noble churches of medieval age.

Photograph by Hallam Ashley

Lincoln Cathedral, West Front

Lincoln Cathedral crowns the highest point in this ancient city with its splendour. It stands on the site of the Roman town where five imperial legionary roads intersected. Paulinus, Bishop of York about 628, brought Christianity to the Saxon town. In 870 it was seized by the Danes and became a centre of their plundering activities. Finally the Normans drove the inhabitants down into the low ground and began the present noble cathedral. The rich door-ways of the splendid fretted west front are as old as 1141, and much of the rest is work begun by the great bishop Hugh of Lincoln in 1192, and completed by his successors in 1280. The exquisite main central and two west towers were added in the next century.

Photograph by A. F. Kersting

Lincoln Cathedral, the Angel Choir

The Angel Choir was designed originally as a shrine in memory of Bishop Hugh, St Hugh of Lincoln (see p. 114), and was much visited by medieval pilgrims. It is the work of Simon of Thirsk, 1256-80, and brings to perfection of proportion the experiments of earlier Norman architects, from which Simon had learnt so much, and improved upon. The clustered shafts supporting the arches and the arcades, the narrow centre bands of the triforium, and the lovely contemporary stained glass fill the visitor with that sense of timeless beauty and reverence which must have inspired the builders themselves. In one of the five bays stands the richly-decorated Easter Sepulchre.

Photograph by A. F. Kersting

Ashness Bridge, Derwentwater

The old pack road from Keswick to Watendlath Tarn and Blea Tarn (120) crosses the arch of little Ashness Bridge, where travellers pause to enjoy once more the changing beauty of the Lakeland scene. Skiddaw (3,054 feet) is due north, above Keswick and the northern half of Derwentwater lake, with its wooded islands and Friar's Crag (122).

Photograph by Kenneth Scowen

Blea Tarn, Westmorland

Of four Blea Tarns in the Lake District one is situated over 1,500 feet up in a deep hollow under Coldbarrow Fell. It can be reached on foot from Thirlmere to the east, or by the wandering footpath from the north through Watendlath valley.

The picture however shows Blea Tarn House in Langdale, where you will see

> *A quiet treeless nook, with two green fields,*
> *A liquid pool that glittered in the sun,*
> *And one bare dwelling, one abode, no more.*

So Wordsworth described it in the *Solitary Valley* of his Excursion—"a lowly vale and yet uplifted high among the mountains". Young larches are growing since Wordsworth described it as treeless, but the sheep and the crags are unchanged and to the north the Langdale Pikes rise as two huge peaks "that from another vale peered into this".

Photograph by Kenneth Scowen

120

Derwentwater, Cumberland

Although ringed around with mountain and fell rising to 3,000 feet, the shallow lake of Derwentwater in the heart of the English Lakes is not more than 244 feet above sea level. It is the broadest though not the longest of them, and diversified with woody islands: Derwent, Lord's and St Herbert's Islands are now protected by the National Trust. The busy little town of Keswick at the northern end of the lake is a good centre for exploring the Lakeland National Park. The road to the south of the town affords fine views of what many visitors consider to be the most enchanting of all the Lakes. On one of the jutting crags here is a bronze medallion head of Ruskin and the inscription: "The first thing I remember as an event in my life was being taken by my nurse to the brow of Friar's Crag on Derwentwater."

Photograph by Kenneth Scowen

122

Thirlmere, Cumberland

The original lake of Thirlmere, 553 feet above sea-level, was raised 34 feet and made half a mile longer by its conversion to use as a reservoir by Manchester Corporation, to which city it now supplies 50 million gallons of water daily through nearly one hundred miles of pipe-line. It is still a very beautiful lake, although its waterline varies more than natural lakes normally do, according to rainfall. Close on the eastern side Helvellyn rises in majestic bareness to 3,118 feet. The western shore is less striking but from its lower slopes rise the formidable Fisher, Raven and Bull Crags. The lake water flows north through picturesque St John's Beck, and eventually joins the Derwent.

Photograph by Kenneth Scowen

Alnwick Castle, Northumberland

Writing in 1567 Clarkson described Alnwick as a "very ancynt large beutifull and portlie castell, scytewate on ye south side of ye river of Alne, upon a lyttle mote". True, it is built on the site of a motte-and-bailey castle. The present castle was begun in the twelfth century, but the walls are mostly fourteenth century. From 1309 it has been continuously occupied by the Percys, Earls of Northumberland. In the eighteenth century the castle was altered by Robert Adam, who decorated it in extreme Gothic style with the approval of the "junketaceous" Percy wife of Sir Hugh Smithson, who became Duke in 1750 after marrying the Percy heiress. Unfortunately Antony Salvin, the fashionable castle-restorer of his day, swept away much of this beauty, 1847-65. The Castle is vast, and part of it is now used as a teachers' training college.

Photograph by Noel Habgood

Robin Hood's Bay, Yorkshire

The romantic red-tiled Robin Hood's Bay village lives on its precarious cliffs by fishing and by taking in summer visitors. At low tide there are fine sands. The Bay sweeps south nearly three miles to Ravenscar, another cliff village. Inland there are miles of glorious moorland rising to nearly 1,000 feet. There are few roads, but many steep lanes and bridle-paths.

Photograph by E. W. Tattersall

The Black Swan, Helmsley, Yorkshire

Helmsley is typical of the pleasant, solid, stone-built larger villages of the North Riding of Yorkshire. Many were founded on the wealth carried on the backs of the dale sheep: wool. Foxes are hunted, for they abound in the hills and valleys of this picturesque region, which is now a National Park. The long beautiful valley of Bilsdale runs north to the Cleveland Hills, and a few miles from Helmsley the ruins of the great Cistercian Abbey of Rievaulx looks down on Rye Dale. It has the earliest large nave in Britain. About 1147-66 there may have been 140 monks and 600 lay brothers—the place swarmed like a hive of bees and sent out colonies from time to time.

Photograph by Trust Houses Ltd

Welsh Ponies

Like this mare in front of the picture, the typical Welsh pony is chestnut or brown-red; but white and parti-coloured, black and palomina individuals are born, though rarely. Their home is the Welsh mountains where they are used to carry Welsh shepherds over the steep and often rocky ground. They are surefooted and extremely hardy, and need no extra feeding in winter except in prolonged snow. They have become popular as mounts for small children. A Welsh Pony Society protects the breed, and many are exported overseas.

This group has been brought down from the Preseli Mountains, Pembrokeshire. Each autumn the free-ranging ponies are rounded up so that the ears of the foals can be notched with the owner's distinguishing mark.

Photograph by Nicholas Meyjes

Tal-y-llyn, Merionethshire

Tal-y-llyn (Head of the Lake) is a hamlet at the western end of a beautiful natural lake (popular with trout fishermen) in the wild rocky heart of mid-Wales. The slopes of Craig Goch (Red Crag) rise steeply behind the inn on the right. To the left is the dark mountain mass of Cader Idris (Chair of Idris, a legendary astronomer who studied the stars from the summit), 2,927 feet high. The lake is over a mile long and fed by streams tumbling out of the screes and *cwms* of the dramatic pass penetrated by the road to Dolgellau. One stream issues from the lofty Llyn-y-cau, a gem-like pool set deep under the cirque of Cader's cliffs, most sombre and lovely of Welsh mountain scenes.

Photograph by John Woolverton

Caernarvon Castle, Caernarvonshire

Caernarvon Castle, partly restored today, is significant in British history as the birthplace of the first (English) Prince of Wales. Edward I, who broke the power of the Welsh princes by ringing Snowdonia with the castles of Conway, Caernarvon, Beaumaris and Harlech, and starving the Llewelyns into submission, proclaimed his son, born at Caernarvon in 1284, as Prince of Wales. The title has ever since been attached to the heir to the Sovereign, who grants it in each case by formal investiture. Begun in 1283, the Castle was sacked by the Welsh in 1294, and invested in 1401, but it remained a stronghold of English power, with its massive and elaborate defences.

Photograph by John Woolverton

136

Princes Street, Edinburgh

Best known of all the streets of Scotland, Princes Street is straight, splendid, seductive, the very heart of Edinburgh's life. On the right-hand (north) side are the fashionable shops, hotels, clubs, restaurants. Opposite, on the left, are the sunny Princes Street Gardens, and the famous Floral Clock. In the foreground is the Sir Walter Scott Memorial, 1840–6, honouring in Gothic style the great novelist. The Royal Scottish Academy is behind. Parallel with Princes Street is the Royal Mile, from Edinburgh Castle on its hill to Holyrood Palace in the glen. The great mass of Arthur's Seat rises 822 feet above sea-level, dominating the capital city of Scotland.

Photograph by A. F. Kersting

The Eildon Hills, Roxburghshire

This is Walter Scott's country, along the Tweed, under the triple peaks of the Eildon or Eldon Hills, all in the lovely rolling border shire of Roxburgh. Fast trout and salmon streams rush down Liddesdale and Teviotdale, well known for their lively scenery. Indeed it is a spirited land, where many border clashes occurred, and around which Scott wrote his novels. Three great but now ruined abbeys should be visited: Jedburgh, 1118; Kelso, 1128; and Melrose, 1136, as well as the many historical houses and other buildings. There is Sandymowe Farm, where Scott spent his youth. He wrote of three towers, those of Branxholm, Darnick and Smailholm. He built Abbotsford House by the Tweed, and worked prodigiously there to wipe out a publishing debt of many thousand pounds, and died there in 1832. The house is open in the summer.

Photograph by Kenneth Scowen

The Forth Bridge

The car ferry leaves South Queensferry for North Queensferry across the Forth estuary. Seawards the great Forth Bridge carries the main railway line between Edinburgh and Perth, Aberdeen and the north of Scotland. The Forth Bridge was built 1883-90. It is 2,765 yards long, with 150 feet clearance for passing ships. The top of the bridge is 361 feet above the sea. The centre pier rest on Inchgarvie Island, and the two centre spans are each 1,710 feet wide. Three men were knighted for the achievement: designers Sir John Fowler and Sir Benjamin Baker, and contractor Sir William Arrol. Today another giant (suspension) bridge has just been completed a little way up river to carry modern road traffic across the Forth.

Photograph by Fred G. Sykes

142

Culross Village, Fife

This neat and charming old fishing village with cobbled streets lies on the north shore of the inner waters of the Forth. It was a Royal Burgh, and at one time extremely busy producing salt in pans along its sunny, south-facing shore. It also made girdles (bakestones). The Scottish National Trust has kept many of its picturesque sixteenth- and seventeenth-century houses in good heart. Note the red-tiled roofs and crow-stepped gables. The old Palace (1597-1611) has panelled and decorated rooms and terraced walled gardens.

Photograph by Kenneth Scowen

Loch Faskally, Pitlochry, Perthshire

Lovely and natural-looking as it lies at the entrance to the southward glen system of the Grampian Mountains, Faskally is in reality an entirely man-made loch, created by the building of the Pitlochry Dam, which feeds the hydro-electric station with the waters of the Tummel. The fine salmon-pass should be visited: visitors can see the fish climbing fifty-four feet up-stream through a series of glass-sided chambers.

Photograph by Kenneth Scowen

The Falls of Dochart, Killin, Perthshire

The silver waters of the River Dochart dance out of the glen under 3,000 feet high mountains on their way to the long reach of Loch Tay. Near Killin they meet the river from Glen Lochay, which tumbles over white falls on its impetuous way. Here stands Finlarig Castle, of Scott's *Fair Maid of Perth*. Amid the ruins of this building is the gruesome relic of feuds and clan warfare, a beheading pit still with its chains, and some carven stones. But the sun shines in the summer, and Killin is popular with climbers and explorers; and the mountain slopes are excellent for winter sports. One of the biggest vines in Europe grows at Kinnell House.

Photograph by Kenneth Scowen

Portree Harbour, Skye

Protected by the long island of Raasay to the east, Portree is the principal harbour of Skye. The inner waters of Raasay Sound often shelter the fishing fleets of the Minch, across which lies the Outer Hebridean fishing centre of Stornoway. The region is beautiful with little islands, mountains rising from the sea, sea-birds, a paradise for naturalist and nature-lover. Whales and basking-sharks, seals, otters, salmon, sea-trout are all here. Near Portree, if not in the town itself, Flora Macdonald said goodbye to ill-fated Prince Charles Edward. At the house (now an hotel) on Raasay Dr Johnson and Boswell were entertained on their famous Hebridean Tour—the irrepressible Boswell climbed to the top of Dun Caen (1,456 feet) and there danced a jig.

Photograph by Kenneth Scowen

Loch Leven and the Peaks of Glencoe

Looking from the north shore of the sparkling sea-way of Loch Leven; the approach to the sombre Glen of Coe ("vale of weeping") turns away inland to the right. On the left is the distinct outline of the Pap of Glencoe (2,430 feet). Snow lies on the ridge of Aonach Eagach (3,168 feet). The waters of sea and burn teem with fish, and it is recorded that the Macdonalds of Glencoe, who suffered the notorious Massacre (p. 154), lived much on salmon, fresh or dried.

Photograph by G. Douglas Bolton

In the Pass of Glencoe

Glencoe! The name is still uttered with bated breath. By nature it is a dark glen of shadows from towering mountains which shut it in, and by clouds which rarely leave its craggy crowns. "The shrouded glen of tears", one writer calls it. But often the sun gleams on Glencoe, and the few inhabitants which still live there are used to the ninety inches of rain and the reproach of ancestral events. It was in 1691 that the secret massacre of the Jacobite clan of Glencoe Macdonalds was planned by their enemy the Master of Stair, Secretary of State, who ordered no quarter even for women and children. On 1st February 1692 men of the King's new Argyll Regiment were quartered on Glencoe on the pretext that the barracks at Fort William were full. They lived hospitably with the clan for a fortnight, then at five in the morning they put the sleeping Macdonalds to the sword and gun. Some of the soldiers were, however, reluctant and half-hearted to carry out the savage order; and the majority escaped. The survivors were resettled with compensation as a result of the public enquiry and indignation which followed.

Photograph by Kenneth Scowen

The Sands of Morar, Argyll

The Sands of Morar are white like snow. They face across the blue water of the Sound of Sleat to the islands of Eigg and Rhum, Inner Hebrides. Just inland lies long Loch Morar, believed to be the deepest (987 feet) in Great Britain. Morar, like Loch Ness, has its own mysterious monster, most often seen, perhaps, when an Atlantic gale is whipping a white water-whirlwind or waterspout across its trout-filled waters, or on calm misty days when mirages occur, and the surrounding mountains are reflected upside down on the deep blue-black waters. Simon Lord Lovat hid in this wild Morar country in 1746; he sought refuge on an island in Loch Morar, where he was at last made prisoner.

Photograph by Kenneth Scowen

In the Cuillins, Skye

One might be in the heart of some grand inland continental mountain range, so steep, naked and inspiring are the Coolins, Cuillins or Cuchullins of Skye. Eagles and red deer find sanctuary here. Yet the sea is nowhere more than a few miles distant in any direction. The Cuillins rise to over 3,000 feet and are composed of dark igneous and crystalline rock, much weathered and softened with lichens. It is fairly solid and reliable for the many climbers who frequent these mountains, although it is possible to get into difficulties if the route is not chosen with care, and sometimes heavy mists completely obscure the path. A compass is not much use owing to the strong magnetic nature of the rock.

Photograph by J. Allan Cash

Loch Maree, Ross

Truly the heart of the Highlands. For stirring beauty and wildness of scenery, and natural wild life, and remoteness from mankind, this region of Wester Ross is unsurpassed. Fortunately for motorists there is a fair road skirting most of the south side of the twelve-mile-long Loch Maree, which turns also around the 10,000-acre National Nature Reserve of Beinn Eighe, at Kinlochewe. The white and grey peaks of quartzite and the red shoulders of Torridon sandstone stand around in majestic grandeur, with often unscaleable cliff. Miles of trackless country are known only to the numerous deer, to the wild cat, the rare pine-marten and the golden eagle. This is a remnant of the original Caledonian Forest.

Photograph by Kenneth Scowen

Quinag, Sutherland

Quinag is 2,653 feet high, on the beautiful, wild, barren, west coast of Sutherland. Just below is the car ferry at Kylesku, where the sea-loch of Cairnbawn flows round the island of Garbh and penetrates by two deep fiords into the heart of mountains rising to 3,273 feet (Ben More Assynt), and compels the wandering road to halt. The scenery is reminiscent of Scandinavian fiordland. Quinag is on the south side of the ferry, and the road slips furtively through rocky bastions and over the boggy glens, one branch going west to Lochinver before joining the other on its way to Inchnadamph. This is a lonely but lovely land, where few crofters survive, where the wild deer and ptarmigan move to the high tops in summer after a winter of sheltering in a hundred roadless glens empty of man.

Photograph by J. Allan Cash

162

The Mountains of Mourne, Co. Down

"The Mountains of Mourne sweep down to the sea", as the song says, and they do, most abruptly, at the high point of Slieve Donard (2,796 feet). There is scarcely room for the coast road, extremely beautiful and wild, between Glassdrummond and Newcastle. There is ever a blue-green light upon the granite slopes of the Mourne Mountains, derived perhaps from this close acquaintance with the Irish Sea. There are little fishing villages along the road and many climbers explore the towering Chimney Rock (2,152 feet).

Tucked away in a glen (the Silent Valley) is a reservoir yielding ten million gallons of water daily to Belfast; the surplus rushes out wildly down the glen until it reaches the tranquil level lands at Kilkeel, which has fine sands and first-class salmon and trout fishing.

Photograph by Kenneth Scowen

164

Port Muck, Co. Antrim

Port Muck on the peninsula of Island Magee gazes across the North Channel to the Galloway shore of Scotland. It is one of the many bewitching little fishing ports which adorn this sheltered shore and are within easy reach of Belfast. The outer world is represented by the regular mail steamer from Stranraer which passes north of Port Muck to Larne, the "main-land" shopping centre for the Magee islanders, who cross the narrow Larne Lough by ferry.

An old castle is in ruins. Just south of Port Muck are the remarkable basaltic cliffs of the Gobbins, 250 feet high. It is alleged that in 1642 the Protestants of Carrickfergus carried out a bloody pogram by hurling hundreds of their prisoners over these cliffs. Two thousand years earlier the Iberians built a megalithic dolmen—a Rocking Stone also belongs to this period.

Photograph by Kenneth Scowen

Narrow Water Castle, Co. Down

This tower commands the narrowing approach to Newry, far up Carlingford Lough, which here divides Ulster or Northern Ireland from Eire. It was the scene of many defensive actions, and was built by the Duke of Ormonde in 1663, after the restoration of Charles II. It dominated the considerable maritime traffic of those days, but is now abandoned and remains a picturesque part of the lovely scenery of an estuary much frequented by yachtsmen and holiday visitors.

Photograph by A. and C. Photography

Enniskillen, Co. Fermanagh

Enniskillen or Inniskilling ("Island of Kathleen") is strategically and beautifully situated between the long Upper and Lower Loughs Erne. It was notorious for its militant Protestantism. The military tradition is strong: two regiments with stirring names and records were recruited here—the Royal Inniskilling Fusiliers and the Inniskilling Dragoons. The Portora Royal School, founded in 1616, is one of the leading public schools of Ireland; Oscar Wilde was a pupil. The curving streets, colour-washed houses above the shop fronts, the clock tower, have a fascination for the visitor. Life is leisurely in far western Fermanagh and there is time to enjoy it. Days can be spent fishing or boating in the maze of bays and small islands of the great Erne loughs. On the Isle of Devenish is the ruins of St Molaise Monastery, and on Inishmacsaint a Celtic abbey; both are sixth century.

Photograph by J. Allan Cash

The coast at Cushendun, Co. Antrim

The coast of Antrim provides some of the loveliest scenery in the British Isles. Cushendun itself is so attractive as it nestles by the sea in its deep glen sheltered from the Atlantic gales that it was purchased by the Ulster Land Fund and given to the National Trust. The gorse-lined lanes and paths climb up and down promontories from one sandy bay to another. The main coast road wanders inland, and above Cushendun crosses a splendid viaduct on its way to Fair Head and the famous Giant's Causeway. Irish Stone Age cultures (back to 6000 B.C.) have been traced in flint tools on the cliffs. Dispossessed Scots invaded this coast and fought many a battle here; proud Shane O'Neill, Earl of Tyrone, was murdered by his host Macdonnel, Earl of Antrim, in 1567, and his body delivered to the English who set his head on a spike at Dublin Castle—a cairn marks the spot at Cushendun.

Photograph by A. and C. Photography

Dunluce Castle, Co. Antrim

Continuing our tale of the ruthless Macdonnels, who had themselves been forced to flee from Scotland, it was this clan which drove the MacUillins from Dunluce Castle in 1558, and made themselves Lords of Antrim. Although this fortress was considered impregnable, as it rests on an islanded rock of basalt, it has a long history of disasters. The first fortress was a Celtic "dun". Exposed to the northwesterly gales of the Atlantic, from time to time portions of cliff and masonry break away when the storm-waves thunder at high tide. It is recorded that during one such storm on a night in 1639 the whole of the kitchen, with eight servants at work inside, crashed into the sea.

Photograph J. Allan Cash